TO

Leslie

Thank you... continue
to rise!

FROM

Louise

MAY YOU BE BLESSED

by KATE NOWAK

simple truths®
THE GIFT OF INSPIRATION

www.simpletruths.com

Published by Simple Truths, LLC
1952 McDowell Road, Suite 300
Naperville, IL 60563-65044

Design: Rich Nickel

Photos:
Steve Terrill (www.terrillphoto.com): pages 63, 64, 67, 68, 76, 92, 99
Bruce Heinemann (www.theartofnature.com): pages 84, 91, 100
Gordon Nickel (www.fallendoor.com): pages 60, 83
Rich Nickel (www.richnickeldesign.com): pages 75, 80, 88, 96

Printed and bound in the United States of America.

ISBN: 978-1-60810-004-0

www.simpletruths.com
(800) 900-3427

09 WOZ 12

Table of Contents

The Story Behind the Blessing

By Kate Nowak

"SOMETIMES OUR LIGHT GOES OUT
BUT IS BLOWN AGAIN INTO FLAME BY AN ENCOUNTER
WITH ANOTHER HUMAN BEING.
EACH OF US OWES THE DEEPEST THANKS
TO THOSE WHO HAVE REKINDLED
THIS INNER LIGHT."

—Albert Schweitzer

It happened a few days after my father's death, in that mind-numbing period of adjustment after someone we love leaves us. Having gone shopping for necessities for my trip back to my own home, I was standing in an otherwise empty aisle of a large chain store when suddenly I sneezed, the last vestiges of an allergy attack I'd fought earlier in the week.

Almost instantly, from the next aisle over I heard a voice call out, "Bless you," and then another, and another, and yet another. All in all, in the span of only a few seconds, I counted eleven different voices coming from every possible direction in the store, some saying "God bless you", others using the word "gezundheit," but all blessing me, all calling good down upon me.

At first I thought little of it. After all the idea of blessing someone when they sneeze is rooted in superstition, an archaic belief that in the act of sneezing the soul is thrown from the body, and a blessing is needed for spiritual protection.

Today, it is usually offered as no more than a courtesy, a polite response that has come to be socially accepted and expected. But on that particular day, in the first few moments following all those blessings being called out to me, I began to notice a difference in myself: A slight shift in perception that left me feeling more connected and empowered than I had in days. It also left me, for the first time since my father's passing, more confident that everything would be all right.

Driving back to my father's house that day, I continued periodic "feelings" checks, marveling at how much stronger I felt. Later, sitting in my parent's kitchen for what would be one of the last times, I recounted the story to my stepmother. "Do you think any of them realized what they were saying?" she asked. "Or was it just out of habit?"

"Just habit," I answered with a shrug, thinking about what a shame it was that people could give such a needed gift as a blessing and not even be aware of what they had done. "It should be a habit, this business of blessing others," I said a moment later. "But it would be nice if people actually knew they could and were making a difference."

A seed was planted that day and two years later it sprouted, awakening me one morning to a gentle soul-whisper that poured forth as the words of a special blessing. Feeling compelled to take pen and paper from my nightstand, I prodded myself into full wakefulness and then sat on the edge of the bed, like a secretary poised for dictation, pen ready to capture each syllable as the inspired words flowed into my awareness.

Because of the power of the internet, those words have since been sent across the planet and read by millions, and as a result, I have received thousands of letters from people telling me how *May You Be Blessed* has impacted their lives. And in each and every instance I have found myself blessed in return.

I have often wondered since if my newfound work as a dispatcher of blessings is the result of a serendipitous accident that placed me in a crowded store on a day when I was both prone to sneeze, and to listen to subtle nudges from the heart. Or was it, perhaps, that my father's gentle spirit was present that day, inspiring others to offer blessings so that I might be lifted up?

Of course, it is a question I cannot answer, but I do know that since that time my life has changed remarkably. Each day is now entirely centered on the act of blessing and I have come to recognize it not only as one of the most powerful and practical ways we have for reconnecting with each other, our world and Life itself, but also the most phenomenal way possible to lead us to happiness and success. It is a discovery I now endeavor daily to share with all.

A blessing, I have come to realize, is a sweet release from pain; a sacred reminder that we are made of love and light and goodness and, as such, part of a greater and most wondrous whole. It is an ancient key to a successful and fulfilling life.

Today, whenever I share with others this phenomenal key, explaining how, as we each develop the habit of blessing others we are blessing our own lives, as well, I feel as if I have been given a wonderful gift. I realize once again how truly blessed I am. It is my hope that as you read this book and allow the words of this blessing to enter your heart, you will be blessed in return. I could not ask for anything sweeter to my soul than that.

This book is lovingly dedicated to my father

Robert Lowell Swanson

September 19, 1926 to October 13, 2003

MAY YOU BE BLESSED
WITH ALL THINGS GOOD.

–Kate Nowak

May you be blessed

with all things good.

May your joys,
like the stars at night,

be too numerous
to count.

May your victories be more abundant

than all the
grains of sand
on all the beaches
on all the oceans
in all the world.

May lack and struggle

only serve to make
you stronger

and may beauty, order and abundance be your constant companions.

May every
pathway
you choose
lead to
that which
is pure
and good
and lovely.

May
every
doubt
and
fear...

...be replaced by
a deep abiding trust
as you behold evidence
of a Higher Power
all around you.

And
when
there is
only
darkness

and the storms of life are closing in...

May the light at the
core of your being

illuminate the world.

May you always
be aware you
are loved
beyond measure
and may you
be willing to
love unconditionally
in return.

May you always
feel protected
and cradled
in the arms
of God,

like the cherished
child you are.

And when you are
tempted to judge,

may you be reminded
that we are all ONE

and that every
thought you think
reverberates across
the universe,
touching everyone
and everything.

And when
you are tempted
to hold back,

may you remember
that love flows best
when it flows freely...

...and it is in giving that we receive

the
greatest
gift.

May you always
have music
and laughter

and may a
rainbow follow
every storm.

May gladness
wash away every
disappointment,

may joy dissolve
every sorrow...

and may love

ease every pain.

May every wound
bring wisdom
and every trial
bring triumph

and with
each passing day
may you live
more abundantly
than the day before.

May you
be blessed.

And may
others
be blessed
by you.

This is my
heartfelt wish
for you.

May you be blessed.

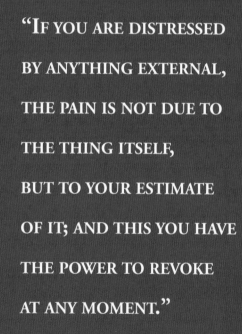

Look for the Blessing

"IF YOU ARE DISTRESSED
BY ANYTHING EXTERNAL,
THE PAIN IS NOT DUE TO
THE THING ITSELF,
BUT TO YOUR ESTIMATE
OF IT; AND THIS YOU HAVE
THE POWER TO REVOKE
AT ANY MOMENT."

—*Marcus Aurelius*

TWO WOMEN WHO HAD BEEN FRIENDS FOR YEARS but had lost touch ran into each other while out shopping one day. In an effort to catch the other up on her life, one of the women said, "We were blessed with the fire in the attic last year. The fire didn't destroy that much, but the water and smoke damage was extensive."

"Why that's terrible!" the other woman replied.

"Oh, no! It was a real blessing," the first woman countered. "You see, the house had been in my husband's family for years and was badly in need of renovation. The fire forced us into doing what we'd been putting off, and once all the repair work was done and we were able to move back in, it was just like moving into a brand new home."

"Oh, I see. I guess that was a blessing after all," the other woman agreed.

"A big one. Then another blessing came when my husband, Jack, tripped over some wire left by one of the contractors and broke his leg in three places."

WE DETERMINE WHETHER
SOMETHING WILL BE A BLESSING
OR A CURSE BY THE WAY WE
CHOOSE TO SEE IT.

MAGICAL THINGS TEND TO HAPPEN
AND THAT WHICH WE LABELED A BLESSING,
MORE OFTEN THAN NOT,
TURNS OUT TO BE ONE.

"Oh, come on now. How could that be a blessing?" the astonished friend asked.

"Because while we were at the hospital getting his leg set, a tornado came and blew the house away."

"Oh, no!" the friend declared, and then a moment later added, "Okay, I understand you were spared, but losing your home like that, why that's nothing short of tragic! I frankly don't see where you find the blessing."

"But that was the biggest blessing of all, you see, because after we cleared away the debris left by the storm, we found a small underground cellar where my husband's grandfather had secretly kept an antique coin collection worth a sizeable fortune. We always knew there was a collection and that it was valuable, but until that tornado revealed it to us, no one ever knew where it was. Now we're rich!"

As the story illustrates, even those experiences we deem calamitous can carry the seeds of a greater blessing. It is often only in retrospect, however, that the benefit reveals itself. And whether or not it reveals itself and how quickly it does so, is dependent upon only one thing: our own individual perspective. *We determine whether something will be a blessing or a curse by the way we choose to see it.*

Life is an ongoing process, and most of us meet something at almost every turn we wish were different. But just because something is not turning out the way we want, doesn't mean it won't. And when we insist on calling it good, when we make up our minds that no matter what, we're going to see it as a blessing, then our minds start working overtime to prove us right. Magical things tend to happen and that which we labeled a blessing, more often than not, turns out to be one.

While the story of the two women may sound far-fetched, we all know people who have suffered tremendous setbacks only to look back years later and declare the experience to have been a blessing. My father, for instance, suffered a massive heart attack while still in his forties. Brought to the brink of death, the attack caused him to re-evaluate every aspect of his life and left him a changed man. Years later, whenever he would talk about that time in his life, it was not the pain and fear he recalled, but

BECOME A HUNTER OF BLESSINGS,
ACTIVELY SEEKING THEM OUT IN EVERY
EXPERIENCE AND PERSON YOU
ENCOUNTER.

LIFE IS TEN PERCENT

WHAT YOU MAKE IT AND

NINETY PERCENT HOW YOU TAKE IT.

—*Ben Franklin*

the challenge it presented and how he had triumphed. To my father, that heart attack was a blessing.

When my friend Jimmy received the devastating news that his board of directors had voted him out of the company he had founded, leaving him with nothing, he had every right to be bitter. No one would have blamed him. Instead, he chose to use the loss as a catapult into a new business venture that is now proving to be more successful than the first.

After being diagnosed with lung cancer, Sandra was told by her doctor to get her affairs in order. Many months later, after she'd proven the doctor wrong and was happily back at work, she leaned toward me one day and said, "You know, I didn't start living until the day the doctor told me I was about to die. I know it sounds funny, but it's like I had to be ready to die before I could figure out how to live." Sandra, too, understood that blessings sometimes arrive in deceptive wrappings.

You have a mind that always tries to be right about everything so you might as well use it to your advantage. Become a hunter of blessings, actively seeking them out in every experience and person you encounter. No matter how bad a situation or person might seem, say to yourself and mean it, "There's a blessing in this, and I will find it!" Your subconscious will accept this statement as a direct order and, if necessary, move heaven and earth to make certain the blessing is found. Follow this regimen for a while and you may very well discover that you've poked a hole in every problem and sent every misery packing. Problems and miseries don't tend to stay in an atmosphere of blessing for very long.

When the apostle James wrote to the members of the early Christian church that they should "count it all joy," he had a good reason for doing so. He understood, as did Benjamin Franklin nearly 2000 years later, that *life is ten percent what you make it and ninety percent how you take it.* And when you take life as a blessing, it tends to become one.

So the next time a difficulty arises, don't let yourself get tied up in knots. Take a deep breath and relax. You have nothing to worry about. That difficulty is nothing more than a signal that a blessing is on its way. And as you start looking for the blessing, everything else will fade away.

MAY YOU FIND
ALL THE BLESSINGS
TUCKED WITHIN THE CREASES AND FOLDS
OF EACH BRAND NEW DAY.

Count Your Blessings

"GRATITUDE UNLOCKS THE FULLNESS OF LIFE.
IT TURNS WHAT WE HAVE INTO ENOUGH, AND MORE.
IT TURNS DENIAL INTO ACCEPTANCE,
CHAOS TO ORDER, AND CONFUSION TO CLARITY.
IT CAN TURN A MEAL INTO A FEAST, A HOUSE INTO A HOME,
A STRANGER INTO A FRIEND.
GRATITUDE MAKES SENSE OF OUR PAST,
BRINGS PEACE FOR TODAY, AND CREATES
A VISION FOR TOMORROW."

—*Melody Beattie*

ONE TEXAS-HOT DAY WHEN I WAS NO MORE THAN FIVE OR SIX, I went with my uncle and two of his friends to pick watermelons. Probably less than an acre in size, the field where the melons grew appeared never-ending to me, every inch of the ground covered in a tangle of vines, with huge, gray-green fruits scattered among the leaves as far as my eyes could see.

As soon as we arrived at the field, one of my uncle's friends pulled an especially big melon from its vine and placed it in a large cooler filled with ice. Then, while I sat watching, perched on top of the cooler in the shade of a nearby tree, the three men harvested the entire field, filling the back of our old truck until the oval fruits were stacked as high as could possibly be without danger of rolling out. Afterwards, while all of us clustered in the shade, my uncle cut open that first melon, now icy cold, and sliced it into segments as big around as dinner plates and as thick as a man's wrist. Further cutting a segment down to a more manageable size, he handed me a piece of the chilled fruit and with juice dripping down my chin and arms, I soon discovered a passion for watermelon that has lasted until this day.

"TODAY I AM GRATEFUL FOR ALL THOSE THINGS THAT GO MISSING BECAUSE THEIR ABSENCE REMINDS ME OF HOW BLESSED I AM TO HAVE HAD THEM AT ALL."

LOOK AT EVERYTHING
AS IF YOU'RE SEEING IT
FOR THE VERY FIRST
AND VERY LAST TIME.

So about a year ago, when I discovered that my local supermarket was carrying little hybridized watermelons, sized just right for one person, I was delighted. I bought one to try, found it perfect; and immediately began adding the little melons to my weekly shopping list. I even wrote about my discovery in my gratitude journal. Having my favorite fruit packaged for one by nature and readily available year around, was, to me, most certainly a blessing worth counting.

Then one day in early February, perhaps six or seven weeks after I'd made my initial discovery, I was doing my weekly grocery shopping, swung my cart down the produce aisle to grab a few of the melons, and found the bin where they'd been kept empty. Wanting to know where they'd been moved, I sought out a stocker. They hadn't been moved, she told me. They had been sold. There would be another shipment arriving later in the week.

Later in the week! I inwardly cried, suddenly feeling like a petulant child being deprived of a favored treat. I didn't want to wait until later in the week. I wanted my favorite little melons NOW!

And then the silliness of my thinking dawned on me. For most of my life, watermelon had been a summer treat only, growing only in those few months of the year when the daily temperatures soar high enough to insure perfect sweetness. Now here I was, in the middle of winter, bemoaning the fact that I couldn't have one. In that instant I realized how quickly I'd stopped counting those melons as a blessing and had started, instead, to take them for granted.

When I left the store a few minutes later, I took out the small notebook and pen I carry in my purse and wrote the date at the top of a blank page. Below that I wrote, "Today I am grateful for all those things that go missing because their absence reminds me of how blessed I am to have had them at all."

Someone quite wise once told me I should *look at everything as if I were seeing it for the very first and very last time.* In a world where we are constantly pushed and prodded into acquiring more and being more, establishing such a mindset has not been easy. I have discovered, however, that when applied wholeheartedly, looking at everything in such a way truly does turn what I have into more than enough.

I thought of this as I left the parking lot that day. I knew I would find those perfect little melons waiting for me the next time I came to the store, and I did. I knew, too, that when once again experienced, I would find the taste of my favorite fruit infinitely sweeter than before, and it was.

Two more blessings for the counting.

MAY YOU ALWAYS HAVE
BLESSINGS TO COUNT,
EVEN IN THOSE TIMES WHEN
THERE DOESN'T APPEAR TO BE ONE.

Judge Not the Blessings

"YOU CAN'T DEPEND
ON YOUR JUDGMENT WHEN
YOUR IMAGINATION IS
OUT OF FOCUS."

—*Mark Twain*

MY FRIEND JACKIE HATED HAVING NANCY AS HER MANAGER. She thought her to be cold, insensitive and overbearing and had, in the past, tried twice to get transferred to another department, but to no avail. Nancy was apparently a favorite with her employers, and since Jackie was both new to the area and the job, she felt she had no strings to pull. This only served to irritate her more.

Then one evening while she was working late to finish up a quarterly report, Jackie felt suddenly sick to her stomach and was on her way to the restroom when she collapsed in the hall. The next thing she knew she was being placed on a gurney and wheeled out to a waiting ambulance. In the sea of faces hovering over her, the only one she recognized was Nancy's, and in the blur of activity, she could feel Nancy squeeze her hand and hear her say, "Don't worry, Jackie, I'm here. I won't leave you."

It was a promise Nancy kept. Over the next few days as Jackie, a newly divorced mother of two, lay in a hospital bed, coming to terms with the damage done by the stroke she had suffered, Nancy not only stopped by to see her two and three times a day, offering never- ending words of encouragement and bringing mail and get-well messages from co-workers, but also stepped in to see that Jackie's two daughters were cared for and

"WHEN WE ARE JUDGING OTHERS,
WE HAVE NO TIME TO LOVE THEM."

—*Mother Teresa*

JUDGING OTHERS DOES NOT LET JOY IN.

that every aspect of Jackie's life was kept running as smoothly as possible in her absence.

When it was necessary for Jackie to leave the hospital and be placed in a rehabilitation facility, Nancy again made all of the arrangements and visited daily, and when Jackie was finally allowed to go home, it was Nancy who made it possible for her to travel to and from physical therapy each day until she was, at last, fully recovered and able to return to work.

By the time I met the two women, over a decade had passed. They still worked for the same company, though Nancy was about to retire, and Jackie was now the manager of her own department, a promotion she had earned the year following her life-changing stroke. It was obvious to everyone that the two women were the best of friends. I was a new hire for the company and learned about their history together when they invited me to lunch.

At Nancy's retirement party a couple of weeks later, I was standing next to Jackie as her dear friend was receiving accolades from the rest of her co-workers. Jackie looked at her and then whispered to me, "Can you believe I used to hate that woman? And if it wasn't for her, I'd probably be dead. Goes to show we never know who among us is an angel, doesn't it?"

None of us really knows about the people we decide to hate. We label them wrong and ourselves right and in so doing never realize that we are building a wall of separation that only grows stronger with time. We truly do block the angels from our midst. It is not until circumstance throws us together, as it did Jackie and Nancy, that we realize how very much we need one another and how very alike we truly are.

As a young girl living with my grandmother, any time I criticized another person in her presence, she would ask to see whose shoes I was wearing, a blunt reminder that unless I'd walked in that person's shoes, I had no right to judge. It was also a signal that I should stop talking and start thinking differently.

Even today, I sometimes catch myself looking down at my feet when I feel tempted to criticize. "Who am I to judge?" I'll ask myself in the next breath, realizing as I do that I have no idea what the target of my critical focus is really going through.

Of course, that doesn't always stop me, and sometimes the judgment tumbles into my thoughts or words and takes up residence before I even notice. But through my own self-experimenting, I have noticed that when I succeed in suspending judgment and allowing myself to look at others from another perspective, my joy increases. ***Judging others, I have discovered, does not let joy in.*** Stepping away from judgment does.

In the long run, all judging others really does is bring pain and block us from our ability to offer love. We were born to give, to bless, and to be a blessing, but when we are sitting in judgment, we can't. As Mother Teresa pointed out, when we are judging others, we have no time to love them. It is only in suspending judgment that we open our hearts to unconditional love and empower ourselves and each other to be the best that we can be.

MAY YOU ALWAYS BE SO BUSY BLESSING THAT YOU HAVE NO TIME TO JUDGE.

The Joy in a
Blessing *Joy*

TAKE HOLD OF YOUR OWN LIFE.
SEE THAT THE WHOLE EXISTENCE
IS CELEBRATING.
THESE TREES ARE NOT SERIOUS,
THESE BIRDS ARE NOT SERIOUS.
THE RIVERS AND THE OCEANS ARE WILD,
AND EVERYWHERE THERE IS FUN,
EVERYWHERE THERE IS JOY AND DELIGHT.
WATCH EXISTENCE,
LISTEN TO THE EXISTENCE
AND BECOME PART OF IT.

— *Osho*

I WAS DRIVING FROM AUSTIN TO MY HOME IN NORTH TEXAS a few months back and stopped for lunch in a small town diner along the way. I had just been seated when an elderly man passed by my table, and catching his toe on the leg of my chair stumbled slightly, grabbing the table for balance.

"Didn't mean to barge in uninvited," he said with a chuckle, "The older my body gets, though, the more it has a mind of its own and sometimes it takes me places I don't intend to go."

I asked if he was certain he was okay and then laughed with him as he cajoled me with another one liner. In a second or two more he was on his way. A few minutes later he stopped by my table again, this time gripping the back of an empty chair and leaning toward me. "My name's Herman, by the way," he said. " I'm 92 years old. I owe my long life to never smoking, never drinking and never chasing women. I might have slid by on the first two, but my wife would have killed me for certain on the third."

Again I laughed and introduced myself. We talked a little longer. Turned out that Herman and his wife were traveling with their daughter, on

JOY IS EVERYWHERE.

JOY IS EVERYWHERE.

their way back home from a family reunion at which he'd received the award for being the oldest and for having traveled the greatest distance. It was easy to see he was proud of the awards.

"Now, we're just driving from town to town," he said, with a gentle shrug, "looking for joy and finding it everywhere we go." He grinned and pushed away from the table, and after giving me a nonchalant wave of his hand, went back to his table.

As I watched Herman rejoin his wife and daughter, I was reminded of the old Zen parable I'd only recently come to understand.

There was once a man who encountered a tiger as he walked across a field. The man fled and the tiger ran after him. Finally coming to a precipice, the man leapt to grab a small bit of vine growing along the chasm wall and hung on to it for dear life. The tiger sniffed at him from above, and when he looked below, he saw another tiger waiting there. He clung even tighter to the vine as two mice scurried down the wall and began nibbling at it. Just then, the man saw a beautiful ripe strawberry growing near him. Grasping the vine with one hand, he reached out and plucked the berry with the other.

It was the sweetest he had ever tasted.

Herman, I realized, was a berry picker. He wasn't worried about hanging on to life. He was having too much fun celebrating joy. Right then and there I determined I'd be a berry picker, too. And for the rest of my trip home, I found myself following Herman's lead and actively looking for joy. I found it peeking back at me almost everywhere I looked. It came in the form of a child's smile at the gas station where I stopped to refuel, and a wisp of snow-white cloud against a sky of pristine blue on a perfect summer day. It came as a wildflower pushing through a crack in concrete to bloom where no flower had ever dared bloom before. It came as the sound of thunder in the distance. And later it came as single raindrop splattered across my windshield, followed by another and another.

It came in countless other ways, as well, as throughout that day, and many since, I was and am reminded that *joy is everywhere and it is only when I refuse to see it that it appears to be absent from my life.*

It came first that day, however, as a beautiful man named Herman who never smoked, never drank and never chased women but always, always remembered to look for joy.

Thank you, my berry-picking friend, wherever you may be.

MAY YOU NEVER FORGET TO LOOK FOR THE JOY.

Forgiving Your Blessings

> "OUT BEYOND
> IDEAS OF WRONGDOING
> AND RIGHT DOING
> THERE IS A FIELD.
> I WILL MEET YOU THERE."
>
> —*Rumi*

JUST BEYOND OUR YARD FENCE IS A CLEARED FIELD EDGED BY DARK WOODS. I can see this field from my study window, and often while seated at my desk, will catch some motion out of the corner of my eye, only to look out the window just in time to see deer moving from the woods into the sunny openness of the field. Heads held high, nostrils testing the air, ears keen to every sound and muscles tensed, these beautiful animals approach the field warily, even the lure of sweet, lush grass unable to override their sense of caution.

While watching the deer one day, it occurred to me that we humans behave much the same way when first we consider forgiving those who have hurt us. Like the deer, we approach with great caution, certain that in deciding to let go of our pain we are putting ourselves at risk. It is our hunger for peace and happiness, however, that beckons us, pulling us past our wariness, into the bright, warm light of this field of love.

As we venture forth into the forgiveness field we begin to understand that forgiving is not something we do for someone else, but a gift we give ourselves. We realize almost immediately that the field is not as fraught with danger as we had feared, nor as filled with complexities as we had

FORGIVING IS
A GIFT WE GIVE
OURSELVES.

STEP INTO THE LIGHT OF A BRIGHT NEW DAY.

assumed. It is, instead, simplicity itself, as simple as stepping first from darkness into dappled shade, and from there into the light of a bright new day.

If the deer never emerged from the dark woods into the bright openness of the field, they might survive, but they would have to adapt to do so. We also adapt when we refuse to come out of the darkness of pain and fear and into the light of love. We harden and become bitter, as inwardly we adjust to the futility of our thinking. The longer we cling to our fears and our hatreds, the more heavy and out of balance we feel. ***It is only in letting go that we return to center.***

We each have our own reasons for not forgiving those who have hurt us. And many times the reasons seem so valid, so totally understandable that the entire world rallies around us and supports us in our unwillingness to forgive. In truth, however, unforgiveness can never be validated because it keeps us from the light. And since light is what we are made of, it is, in essence, keeping us from ourselves.

Forgiving is not as difficult as most would think. It is as much an act of the imagination as it is anything. It dares us to think of a brighter future, one where no boundaries of right and wrong exist, but only openness and the freedom to be who we truly are. Perhaps most importantly, though, it allows us to go to a place in our hearts where pain and suffering are no longer allowed to have the final word.

MAY YOU ALWAYS BE WILLING
TO STEP FROM THE DARKNESS OF FEAR
INTO THE FIELD OF LIGHT
THAT IS FORGIVENESS.

A Dispatcher of Blessings

"FOR THOSE TO WHOM MUCH IS GIVEN, MUCH IS REQUIRED."

—*John Fitzgerald Kennedy*

WHEN OUR FIRST CHILD WAS BORN I BECAME A NERVOUS WRECK. I worried constantly that something would go wrong. She was so little and helpless and had most certainly not come with an instruction manual. I was young, had had little experience with infants, and, frankly, felt more capable of flying to the moon than of taking care of this tiny being.

When she was about three weeks old, a carpenter came to do some needed repairs on our house and brought his wife with him. While her husband worked, the wife, who had raised three children and was a grandmother of four, watched as I fretted over the baby. I confided that I lived in constant fear that something would happen to this precious child who had been entrusted to me, and had no idea how I was going to cope as she grew older and I had even less control.

"Honey, you're just going to have to bless that child and let her go," the woman advised. It was some of the best advice I ever received.

From that day forward, I wrapped my daughter in blessings when I woke up every morning and before I went to sleep at night. I did the same

WRAP YOUR
LOVED ONES
WITH BLESSINGS
OF WELLNESS
AND JOY.

with my husband and when my sons were born, I wrapped them in blessings, too. It became a habit that has remained with me over the years.

At first the blessings were for protection, but later as my children grew, I began imagining my children and all those I loved, for that matter, being blessed with wellness and joy. I imagined them each surrounded by angels, protected and loved and utterly cared for in every way.

I don't know for certain that my blessings have made a difference, but in my heart I think they have. And I do know they've made a difference in me. *Through this simple act of blessing I've been able to transform myself from being a worrier to a warrior for good,* my weaponry a saber of light and love deftly slicing through my imaginings, removing every vestige of fear and concern. Blessing those I love fills me with a sense of completion, a knowing that in relinquishing my own personal need for control and surrounding them with energy far greater than my own, I have done all I can possibly do.

About the Author

Author Kate Nowak leads a joyfully simplistic life in rural Texas where, surrounded by friends, family and bountiful blessings of the most wonderful sort, she lives with her husband of 40-plus years, a cluster of farm animals far too domesticated for any real farm to claim, and two outrageously spoiled dogs.

Believing the quickest way to right the world is by honoring what is already right, Kate strives daily to be an active dispatcher of blessings by incorporating the blessing process into every facet of her life. Through participation in her world-wide blessing experiment, she also encourages others to do the same and offers instruction in living what she lovingly refers to as the "Blessing Way."

Using the internet to help broadcast her message, Kate challenges visitors to her site to spend just 30 days blessing the world instead of being stressed by it, guaranteeing it to be a life-transforming experience. For more information about the experiment and challenge or to learn more about why she truly believes it is *always better to bless,* Kate invites you to visit her interactive blessing community at **www.bettertobless.com**

I now enjoy thinking of myself as being a dispatcher of blessings, and I encourage you to become one, too. Dispatch blessings to your friends and loved ones daily. Surround them in good thoughts as you go about your day. It may not make a difference, but it most certainly won't do any harm.

In fact I encourage you to send blessings to everyone you meet, and even to those who only come to mind. It takes very little effort to send a good thought, after all, and when you lift those around you up in blessing, you may very well be making a far greater difference in this world than you will ever know.

MAY WE ALL COME TO LIVE
IN A WORLD WHERE EVERYONE IS BLESSED
BY THE PRESENCE OF EVERYONE ELSE...

MAY WE ALL COME TO KNOW JUST HOW
BEAUTIFUL SUCH A WORLD CAN BE.